chicken

simple and delicious easy-to-make recipes

Jean May

This is a Parragon Publishing Book
First published in 2002

Parragon Publishing
Queen Street House
4 Queen Street
Bath, BA1 1HE, UK

Titles in this series are subject to availability

ISBN: 0-75258-867-2

Printed in China

Produced by the Bridgewater Book Company Ltd.

Photographer Calvey Taylor-Haw

Home Economist Ruth Pollock

NOTES FOR THE READER

- This book uses both imperial and metric measurements. Follow the same units of measurement throughout; do not mix imperial and metric.

- All spoon measurements are level: teaspoons are assumed to be 5 ml, and tablespoons are assumed to be 15 ml.

- Unless otherwise stated, milk is assumed to be whole milk, eggs and individual vegetables such as potatoes are medium, and pepper is freshly ground black pepper.

- Recipes using raw or very lightly cooked eggs should be avoided by infants, the elderly, pregnant women, convalescents, and anyone suffering from an illness.

- The times given are an approximate guide only. Preparation times differ according to the techniques used by different people and the cooking times may also vary from those given. Optional ingredients, variations, or serving suggestions have not been included in the calculations.

contents

introduction

Chicken is marvelously versatile and its popularity never seems to wane. From succulent appetizers and snacks to full traditional roast meals, this delicately flavored bird can provide a host of tantalizing dishes for every occasion. Whether that occasion is a simple lunch or an extravagant dinner party, a buffet, barbecue grill, picnic, or supper, the practical yet delicious versatility of chicken will always come into its own.

For the health-conscious among you, chicken is amazingly low in fat, especially when cooked without the skin. It is also extremely nutritious. Chicken is rich in protein and B vitamins, especially vitamin B3, which promotes healthy skin and digestion, boosts energy, and helps to lower cholesterol. Chicken is also an excellent source of magnesium, which helps to fight stress and depression and protects against heart attacks.

On the flavor front, chicken combines well with so many delicious foods that the possible combinations are endless. It is also inexpensive, and a little can go a long way. So what better way to capitalize on the marvelous benefits of chicken than by sampling the recipes in this book? Whatever the occasion, there is bound to be something in the following pages to suit every taste and every budget.

guide to recipe key	
very easy	Recipes are graded as follows: 1 pea = easy; 2 peas = very easy; 3 peas = extremely easy.
serves 4	Recipes generally serve four people. Simply halve the ingredients to serve two, taking care not to mix imperial and metric measurements.
10 minutes	Preparation time. Where marinating or soaking are involved, these times have been added on separately: eg, 15 minutes + 30 minutes to marinate.
10 minutes	Cooking time. Cooking times do not include the cooking of side dishes or accompaniments served with the main dishes.

chicken & shrimp laksa
page 14

chicken with creamy spaghetti
page 42

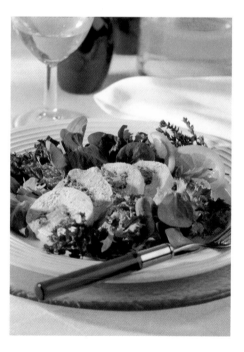

chicken & barley stew
page 70

chicken pinwheels with
blue cheese & herbs, page 92

soups
& appetizers

Making soup at home is quick, easy, and satisfying, and an economical way of using leftover chicken. The soups in this section reflect the delightful flavors of international cuisine, such as the Thai Chicken Soup, which evokes the unforgettable flavors of Thailand, and the delicious Scottish Cock-a-Leekie, a comforting soup for cold days and nights. This section also features some very tempting appetizers, such as succulent Bread-Crumbed Chicken Morsels, and sumptuous Chicken Livers in Red Wine & Thyme.

thai chicken soup

very easy	
serves 4	
15–20 minutes	
30 minutes	

ingredients

1 tbsp sesame oil or chili oil
2 garlic cloves, chopped
2 scallions, trimmed and sliced
1 leek, trimmed and finely sliced
1 tbsp grated fresh gingerroot
1 red chile, seeded and finely chopped
12 oz/350 g skinless chicken breasts,
   cut into strips

scant 3½ cups chicken bouillon
2 tbsp rice wine
1 tbsp chopped lemongrass
6 kaffir lime leaves, finely shredded
7 oz/200 g fine egg noodles
salt and pepper

Heat the oil in a wok or large pan. Add the garlic and cook over medium heat, stirring, for 1 minute, then add the scallions, leek, gingerroot, and chile and cook, stirring, for another 3 minutes. Add the chicken strips, bouillon, and rice wine, bring to a boil, and simmer for 20 minutes. Stir in the lemongrass and lime leaves.

Bring a separate pan of water to a boil and add the noodles. Cook for 3 minutes, drain well, then add them to the soup. Season with salt and pepper. Cook for another 2 minutes. Remove from the heat, ladle into individual bowls, and serve hot.

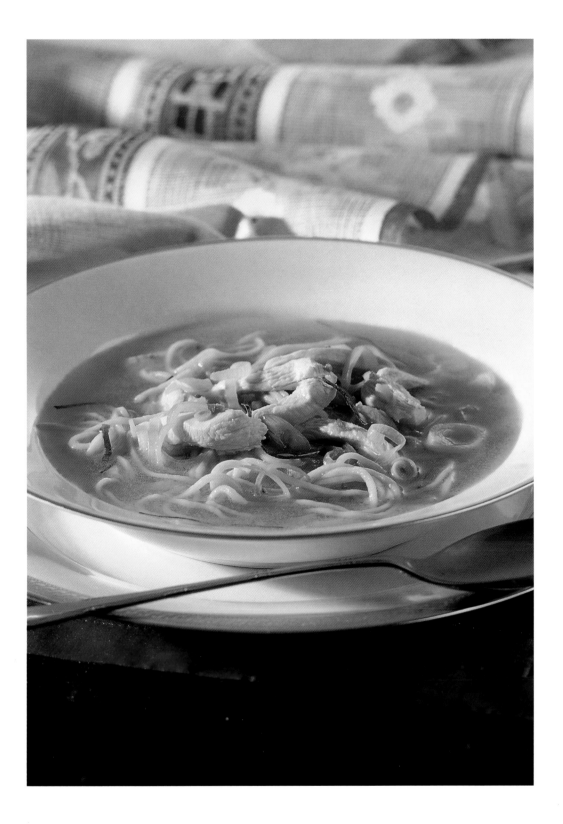

cilantro chicken soup

		ingredients	
very easy		1 tbsp sunflower oil	3 oz/85 g fresh oyster
		1 garlic clove, finely chopped	mushrooms, sliced
		6 shallots, chopped	1¼ oz/35 g fresh cilantro
serves 4		2 scallions, trimmed and finely sliced	leaves, chopped
		1 tbsp grated fresh gingerroot	1 tbsp Thai fish sauce
15–20 minutes		1 small red chile, seeded and	1 tbsp grated lemon zest
		finely chopped	2 tbsp lemon juice
		10½ oz/300 g skinless chicken breasts,	1 tbsp chopped fresh lemongrass
		cut into strips	salt and pepper
30 minutes		4 cups chicken bouillon	1¾ cups bean sprouts

Heat the sunflower oil in a wok or large pan. Add the garlic and cook over medium heat, stirring, for 1 minute, then add the shallots, scallions, gingerroot, and chile and cook, stirring, for another 3 minutes. Add the chicken strips, bouillon, mushrooms, and cilantro, and bring to a boil. Lower the heat and stir in the fish sauce and the lemon zest and juice. Simmer for 20 minutes.

Stir in the lemongrass and season with salt and pepper. Cook for about 2 minutes, then add the bean sprouts. Cook for another minute, then remove from the heat, ladle into individual bowls, and serve hot.

cock-a-leekie

	ingredients	
easy	4 leeks, trimmed	GARNISH
	1 small whole chicken, ready	12 whole cooked prunes, pitted
	for boiling	1 tbsp chopped fresh parsley
serves 4	4 strips lean bacon	
	2 tbsp chopped fresh parsley	
	1 tbsp chopped fresh thyme	
15–20 minutes	1 bay leaf	
	6¼ cups water	
	salt and pepper	
3 hours	generous ¾ cup heavy cream	

Chop the leeks and put them into a large pot with the chicken, bacon, herbs, and water. Season with salt and pepper. Bring to a boil, then lower the heat, cover the pan, and simmer for about 2¾ hours, topping up the water level when necessary.

Remove from the heat and strain the soup into a large bowl. Remove the flesh from the chicken, cut into strips and add to the bowl. Discard the carcass. Cut the bacon into strips and add to the bowl with the chicken meat. Return the soup to the pot and add the rest of the leeks. Bring back to a boil, then lower the heat and simmer for 15 minutes. Stir in the cream and warm through gently, then remove from the heat and ladle into individual bowls. Garnish with whole prunes and chopped parsley and serve.

chicken & shrimp laksa

		ingredients	
very easy	1 tbsp sesame oil	2 tbsp chopped fresh cilantro
	3 scallions, trimmed and sliced	salt and pepper
serves 4	2 tbsp Thai red curry paste	8 oz/225 g vermicelli
	1 tbsp cornstarch	7 oz/200 g cooked shrimp, peeled
	2 tbsp coconut milk	1½ cups evaporated milk
15 minutes	scant 2 cups chicken bouillon	1¾ cups bean sprouts
	11½ oz/325 g skinless chicken breasts, cut into strips	chopped fresh cilantro, to garnish
30 minutes		

Heat the oil in a wok or large pan. Add the scallions and cook, stirring, for 2 minutes. Add the curry paste and cook for another minute. Stir in the cornstarch and coconut milk, then add the bouillon, chicken strips, and cilantro. Season with salt and pepper. Bring to a boil, then lower the heat, cover the pan, and simmer for 20 minutes.

About halfway through the cooking time, bring a pan of lightly salted water to a boil and add the vermicelli. Cook over medium heat for about 10 minutes if using dried pasta, or 4 minutes if using fresh (check the instructions on the package), until tender but still firm to the bite. Remove from the heat, drain, and divide between 4 soup bowls. Add the shrimp and evaporated milk to the chicken mixture and cook for 1 minute. Add the bean sprouts, cook for another minute, then remove from the heat. Ladle the mixture over the vermicelli, garnish with cilantro, and serve hot.

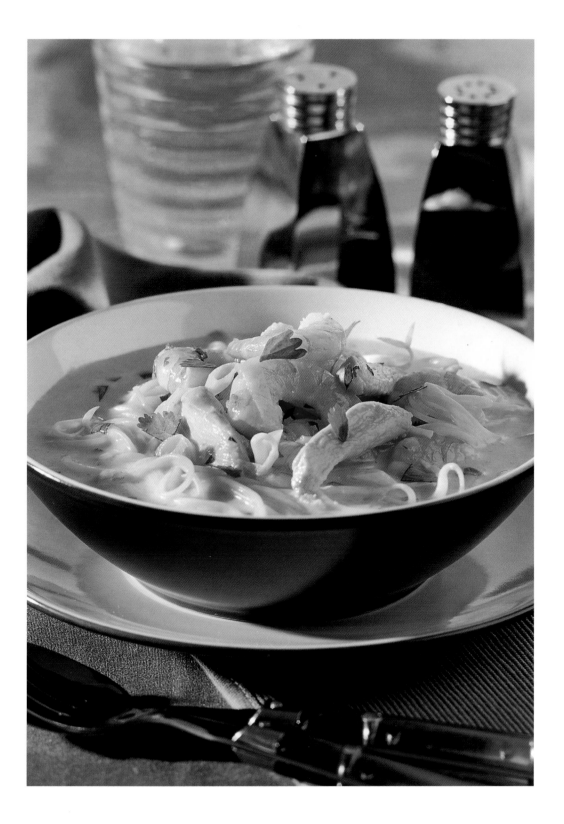

bread-crumbed chicken morsels

		ingredients	
	very easy	1¾ cups fresh white or whole-wheat bread crumbs 3 tbsp grated romano cheese 1 tbsp dried mixed herbs salt and pepper 1 egg 4 skinless chicken breasts, cut into thick strips TARTARE SAUCE generous ¾ cup mayonnaise	1 tbsp lemon juice 2 tbsp chopped fresh chives 1 garlic clove, finely chopped 1 tbsp capers, chopped 2 shallots, finely chopped 1¾ oz/50 g dill pickles, chopped 6 black olives, pitted and finely chopped wedges of lemon, to garnish fresh mixed salad greens, to serve
	serves 4		
	20 minutes		
	30 minutes		

Preheat the oven to 400°F/200°C. Put the bread crumbs into a large, shallow bowl. Add the romano cheese and mixed herbs and season well with salt and pepper. Mix together well. Beat the egg in a separate bowl. Dip the chicken strips into the beaten egg, then coat them in the bread crumb mixture. Arrange on a cookie sheet, then transfer to the preheated oven. Bake for 30 minutes until golden.

Meanwhile, to make the tartare sauce, put the mayonnaise into a bowl and stir in the lemon juice and chives. Add the garlic, capers, shallots, dill pickles, and olives and mix together well.

Arrange the mixed salad greens on a large serving platter. Remove the chicken from the oven and arrange over the salad greens. Garnish with lemon wedges and serve with the tartare sauce.

chicken crostini

		ingredients	
very easy		12 slices French bread or rustic bread	4 tomatoes, sliced
		4 tbsp olive oil	12 thin slices of goat cheese
serves 4		2 garlic cloves, chopped	12 black olives, pitted and chopped
		2 tbsp finely chopped fresh oregano	
		salt and pepper	fresh red and green lettuce leaves,
15 minutes		3½ oz/100 g cold roast chicken, cut	to serve
		into small, thin slices	
10 minutes			

Preheat the oven to 350°F/180°C and the broiler to medium. Put the bread under the preheated broiler and lightly toast on both sides. Meanwhile, pour the olive oil into a bowl and add the garlic and oregano. Season with salt and pepper and mix well. Remove the toasted bread slices from the broiler and brush them on one side only with the oil mixture.

Place the bread slices, oiled sides up, on a cookie sheet. Put some sliced chicken on top of each one, followed by a slice of tomato. Divide the slices of goat cheese between them, then top with the chopped olives. Drizzle over the remaining oil mixture and transfer to the preheated oven. Bake for about 5 minutes, or until the cheese is golden and starting to melt. Remove from the oven and serve on a bed of fresh red and green lettuce leaves.

spicy chicken dippers

		ingredients	
very easy	1¾ cups fresh white or whole-wheat bread crumbs		1 tbsp tomato paste
			1 small red chile, seeded and finely chopped
serves 4	3 tbsp freshly grated Parmesan cheese		1 large tomato, seeded and finely chopped
	1 tsp chili powder		
	salt and pepper		2 tbsp finely chopped peeled cucumber
15–20 minutes	1 egg		
	4 skinless chicken breasts, cut into thick strips		cherry tomatoes, halved, to garnish
	SPICY TOMATO DIP		TO SERVE
30 minutes	3½ oz/100 g cream cheese		fresh salad greens
			celery and carrots, cut into thick sticks

Preheat the oven to 400°F/200°C. Put the bread crumbs into a large, shallow bowl. Add the Parmesan and chili powder, season with salt and pepper, and mix well. Beat the egg in a separate bowl. Dip the chicken strips into the egg, then coat them in the bread crumb mixture. Arrange on a cookie sheet and transfer to the preheated oven. Bake for 30 minutes until golden.

Meanwhile, to make the dip, put the cream cheese into a bowl and stir in the tomato paste. Add the chile, tomato, and cucumber and mix together well.

Arrange the salad greens on a large serving platter. Remove the chicken from the oven and arrange over the salad greens. Garnish with cherry tomatoes and serve with the celery and carrot sticks and the spicy tomato dip.

chicken livers in
red wine & thyme

extremely easy	
serves 4	
10 minutes	
5 minutes	

ingredients

9 oz/250 g fresh chicken livers
3 tbsp lemon-flavored oil
2 garlic cloves, finely chopped
4 tbsp red wine
1 tbsp chopped fresh thyme
salt and pepper

sprigs of fresh thyme, to garnish

TO SERVE
arugula leaves
fresh crusty bread

Rinse the chicken livers under cold running water and pat dry with paper towels. Heat the lemon-flavored oil in a skillet. Add the garlic and cook, stirring, over medium heat for 2 minutes. Add the chicken livers, wine, and thyme. Season with salt and pepper and cook for 3 minutes.

Meanwhile, arrange the arugula leaves on a large serving platter. Remove the pan from the heat and spoon the chicken livers over the bed of arugula. Pour over the cooking juices, then garnish with sprigs of fresh thyme and serve with fresh crusty bread.

salads &
light meals

This section is crammed with delicious salads, snacks, and light meals to tempt the taste buds. From Chicken, Cheese & Arugula salad to mouthwatering Buttered Chicken Parcels, and from Chicken with Creamy Spaghetti to Chicken in Cranberry & Red Wine Sauce, these dishes will be irresistible. In fact, if you find that there is never enough of these lighter dishes to go round, why not serve them as an entrée? Just add some substantial accompaniments, such as crusty bread or freshly cooked rice or potatoes, and you will have a complete and satisfying meal.

thai-style chicken salad

		ingredients	
extremely easy		14 oz/400 g small new potatoes, scrubbed and cut in half, lengthwise	DRESSING
		7 oz/200 g baby corn cobs, sliced	6 tbsp chili oil or sesame oil
serves 4		1½ cups bean sprouts	2 tbsp lime juice
		3 scallions, trimmed and sliced	1 tbsp light soy sauce
		4 cooked, skinless chicken breasts, sliced	1 tbsp chopped fresh cilantro
15 minutes		1 tbsp chopped lemongrass	1 small, red chile, seeded and finely chopped
		2 tbsp chopped fresh cilantro	GARNISH
20 minutes		salt and pepper	wedges of lime
			fresh cilantro leaves

Bring two pans of water to the boil. Put the potatoes into one pan and cook for 15 minutes until tender. Put the corn cobs into the other pan and cook for 5 minutes until tender. Drain the potatoes and corn cobs well and let cool.

When the vegetables are cool, transfer them into a large serving dish. Add the bean sprouts, scallions, chicken, lemongrass, and cilantro and season with salt and pepper.

To make the dressing, put all the ingredients into a screw-top jar and shake well. Alternatively, put them into a bowl and mix together well. Drizzle the dressing over the salad and garnish with lime wedges and cilantro leaves. Serve at once.

chicken, cheese & arugula salad

		ingredients	

	extremely easy	5½ oz/150 g arugula leaves
		2 celery stalks, trimmed and sliced
		½ cucumber, sliced
		2 scallions, trimmed and sliced
		2 tbsp chopped fresh parsley
		1 oz/25 g walnut pieces
		12 oz/350 g boneless roast
		  chicken, sliced
		4½ oz/125 g Stilton cheese, cubed
			handful of seedless red grapes,
			  cut in half (optional)
			salt and pepper
			
			DRESSING
			2 tbsp olive oil
			1 tbsp sherry vinegar
			1 tsp Dijon mustard
			1 tbsp chopped mixed herbs

	serves 4		
	15 minutes		
	—		

Wash the arugula leaves, pat dry with paper towels, and put them into a large salad bowl. Add the celery, cucumber, scallions, parsley, and walnuts and mix together well. Transfer onto a large serving platter. Arrange the chicken slices over the salad, then scatter over the cheese. Add the red grapes, if using. Season well with salt and pepper.

To make the dressing, put all the ingredients into a screw-top jar and shake well. Alternatively, put them into a bowl and mix together well. Drizzle the dressing over the salad and serve.

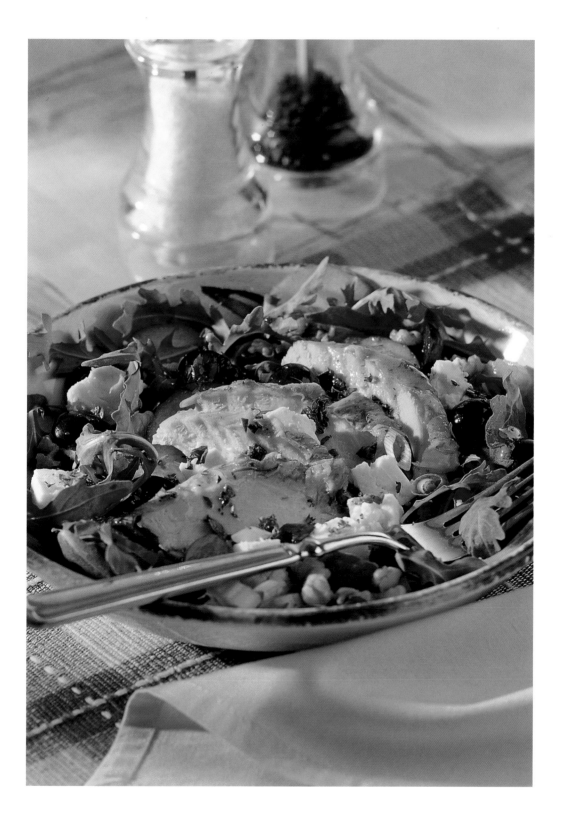

sage & onion drumsticks

		ingredients	
	very easy	6 tbsp butter	8 large chicken drumsticks
		1 onion, finely chopped	2 eggs, beaten
	serves 4	1 garlic clove, finely chopped	3 tbsp vegetable oil
		2½ cups fresh white or	
		whole-wheat bread crumbs	GARNISH
		2 tbsp finely chopped fresh sage	wedges of lemon
	25 minutes	1 tbsp lemon juice	sprigs of fresh flatleaf parsley
		salt and pepper	
			fresh salad greens, to serve
	55 minutes		

Preheat the oven to 400°F/200°C. Melt the butter in a skillet over medium heat. Add the onion and garlic and cook, stirring, for 3 minutes. Remove from the heat and stir in the bread crumbs, sage, and lemon juice. Season well with salt and pepper. Transfer to a large bowl.

Rinse the drumsticks and pat dry with paper towels. Turn the drumsticks in the beaten egg, then coat them in the sage and onion mixture by pressing it around them. Arrange them in a shallow roasting pan, drizzle over the oil, then roast them in the preheated oven for about 50 minutes until golden and crispy and cooked right through. If they start to brown too quickly, cover the roasting pan with foil. Remove from the oven and pile onto a serving platter. Garnish with lemon wedges and sprigs of fresh flatleaf parsley and serve with salad. Alternatively, to serve cold, let cool, cover with plastic wrap, and refrigerate until required.

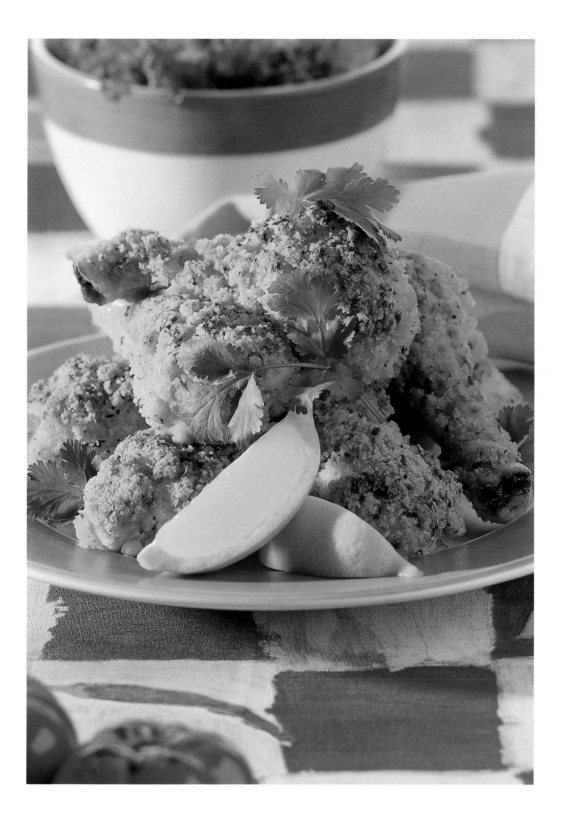

buttered chicken parcels

		ingredients	
	easy	4 tbsp butter	1 tbsp chopped fresh oregano
		4 shallots, finely chopped	pepper
	serves 4	10½ oz/300 g frozen spinach, thawed	4 large, skinless chicken breasts
		1 lb/450 g blue cheese, such as	8 slices prosciutto
		Stilton, crumbled	fresh chives, to garnish
	15–20 minutes + 10 minutes to cool	1 egg, lightly beaten	
		1 tbsp chopped fresh chives	baby spinach leaves, to serve
	35 minutes		

Melt half of the butter in a skillet over medium heat. Add the shallots and cook, stirring, for 4 minutes. Remove from the heat and let cool for 10 minutes.

Preheat the oven to 350°F/180°C. Using your hands, squeeze out as much moisture from the thawed spinach as possible. Transfer the spinach into a large bowl, add the shallots, cheese, egg, herbs, and seasoning. Mix together well.

Halve each chicken breast and pound lightly to flatten each piece. Spoon some cheese mixture into the center of each piece, then roll them up. Wrap each roll in a slice of prosciutto and secure with a toothpick. Transfer to a roasting dish and dot with the remaining butter. Bake in the preheated oven for 30 minutes until golden.

Divide the baby spinach leaves between 4 serving plates. Remove the chicken from the oven and place 2 chicken rolls on each bed of spinach. Garnish with fresh chives and serve.

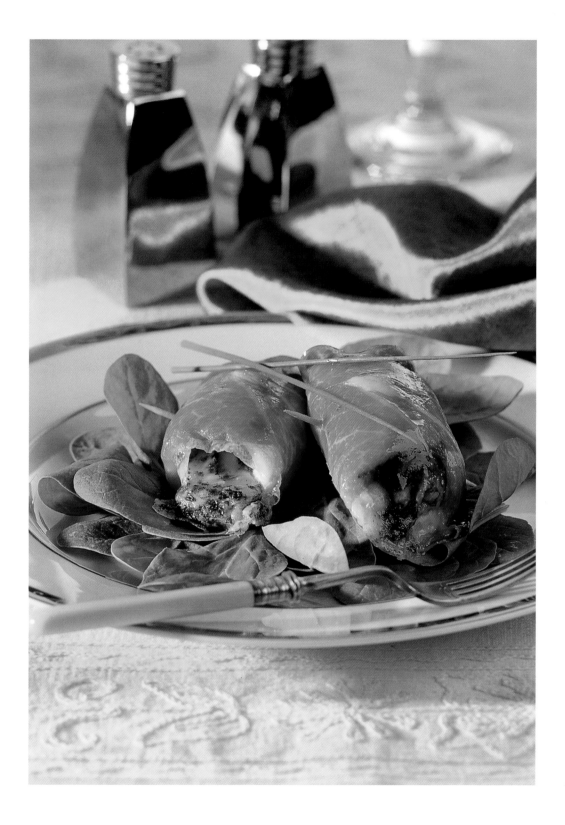

crispy coated chicken breasts

		ingredients	
easy		**SWEET POTATO WEDGES**	2 tbsp freshly grated romano cheese
		4 large sweet potatoes, peeled and	1 tbsp chopped fresh parsley
serves 4		cut into wedges	salt and pepper
		4 tbsp vegetable oil	4 skinless chicken breasts
		1 tsp chili powder	1 egg, beaten
15–20 minutes		1¾ oz/50 g hazelnuts, toasted	4 tbsp vegetable oil
		and ground	
		3 tbsp dried white or	sprigs of fresh flatleaf parsley,
45–55 minutes		whole-wheat bread crumbs	to garnish
			wedges of lemon, to serve

Preheat the oven to 400°F/200°C. To make the potato wedges, bring a large pan of water to a boil. Add the potatoes and cook over medium heat for 5 minutes. Drain well. Pour 2 tablespoons of the oil into a large bowl and stir in the chili powder. Add the potatoes and turn in the mixture until coated. Transfer to a cookie sheet, drizzle over the remaining oil, and bake for 35–40 minutes, turning frequently, until golden and cooked through.

About 15 minutes before the end of the cooking time, put the hazelnuts, bread crumbs, cheese, and parsley into a bowl, season, and mix. Dip the chicken breasts into the egg, then coat in the bread crumb mixture. Heat the oil in a skillet. Add the chicken and cook over medium heat for 3–4 minutes on each side until golden. Lift out and drain on paper towels. Remove the potatoes from the oven, divide between 4 serving plates, and add a chicken breast to each. Garnish with parsley and serve with lemon wedges.

chicken kiev

		ingredients	
easy		4 tbsp butter, softened	3 tbsp freshly grated Parmesan cheese
		1 garlic clove, finely chopped	1 egg, beaten
serves 4		1 tbsp finely chopped fresh parsley	
		1 tbsp finely chopped fresh oregano	GARNISH
		salt and pepper	slices of lemon
		4 skinless chicken breasts	sprigs of fresh flatleaf parsley
20 minutes		generous 1 cup vegetable oil, for	
		deep-frying	TO SERVE
		1¾ cups fresh white or	freshly cooked new potatoes
5 minutes		whole-wheat bread crumbs	selection of cooked vegetables

Put the butter and garlic into a bowl and mix together well. Stir in the chopped herbs and season well with salt and pepper. Pound the chicken breasts to flatten them, then put a tablespoon of herb butter in the center of each one. Fold in the sides to enclose the butter, then secure with toothpicks.

Pour oil into a pan to a depth that will cover the chicken parcels. Heat until very hot. Meanwhile, combine the bread crumbs and grated Parmesan on a plate. Dip the chicken parcels into the beaten egg, then coat in the bread crumb mixture. Transfer the chicken to the hot oil and cook for 5 minutes, or until cooked through. Lift out the chicken and drain on paper towels. Divide the chicken between 4 serving plates, garnish with lemon slices and sprigs of fresh flatleaf parsley, and serve with new potatoes and a selection of vegetables.

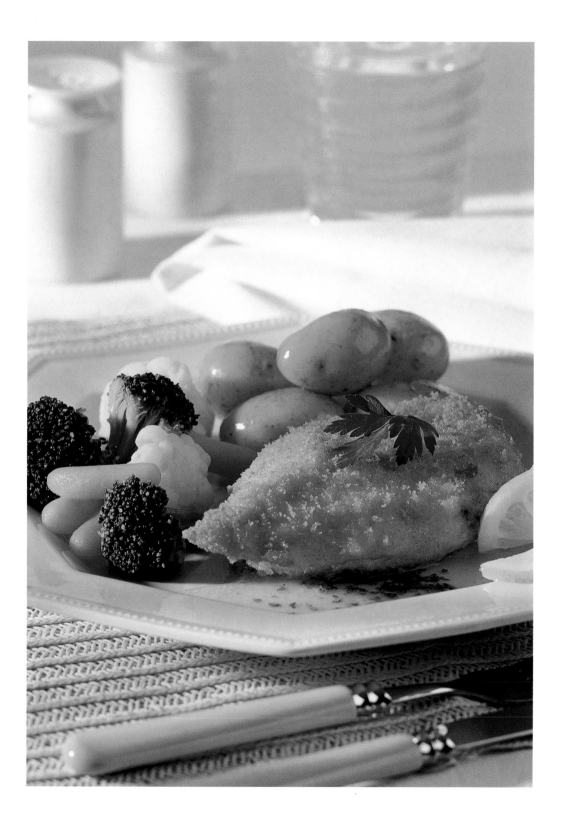

chicken & peanut stir-fry

		ingredients	
very easy		2 tbsp peanut oil	5½ oz/150 g sugar snap peas, trimmed
		1 garlic clove, chopped	4½ oz/125 g baby corn cobs
serves 4		3 scallions, trimmed and sliced	2 tbsp smooth peanut butter
		4 skinless chicken breasts, cut into	1 tbsp light soy sauce
		bite-size chunks	
		1 tbsp grated fresh gingerroot	TO SERVE
15 minutes		½ tsp chili powder	freshly cooked brown or white rice
			fresh green and red salad leaves
8–9 minutes			

Heat the oil in a preheated wok or large skillet. Add the garlic and scallions and stir-fry over medium-high heat for 1 minute. Add the chicken pieces, gingerroot, and chili powder and stir-fry for 4 minutes. Add the sugar snap peas and baby corn cobs and cook for 2 minutes.

In a bowl, mix together the peanut butter and soy sauce, then add it to the wok. Stir-fry for another minute. Remove from the heat, pile onto 4 serving plates, and serve with freshly cooked rice.

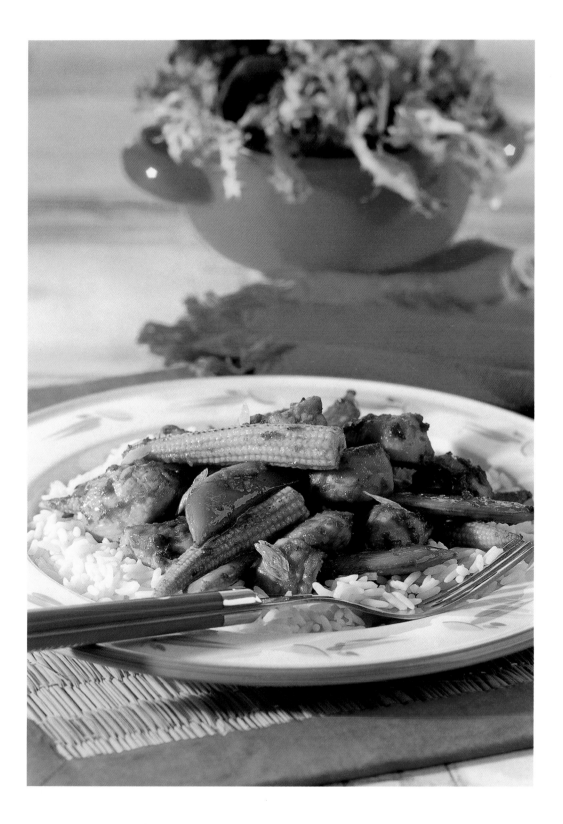

five-spice chicken
with vegetables

		ingredients	
✎	very easy	2 tbsp sesame oil 1 garlic clove, chopped	1 tbsp grated fresh gingerroot ½ cup chicken bouillon
⫻	serves 4	3 scallions, trimmed and sliced 1 tbsp cornstarch 2 tbsp rice wine	3½ oz/100 g baby corn cobs, sliced 3 cups bean sprouts
◡	15 minutes	4 skinless chicken breasts, cut into strips 1 tbsp Chinese five-spice powder	finely chopped scallions, to garnish, optional freshly cooked jasmine rice, to serve
◔	9–10 minutes		

Heat the oil in a preheated wok or large skillet. Add the garlic and scallions and stir-fry over medium-high heat for 1 minute.

In a bowl, mix together the cornstarch and rice wine, then add the mixture to the pan. Stir-fry for 1 minute, then add the chicken, five-spice powder, gingerroot, and chicken bouillon and cook for another 4 minutes. Add the corn cobs and cook for 2 minutes, then add the bean sprouts and cook for another minute.

Remove from the heat, garnish with chopped scallions, if using, and serve with freshly cooked jasmine rice.

chicken with creamy spaghetti

		ingredients	
very easy		MARINADE	salt and pepper
		2 tbsp olive oil	2 tbsp olive oil
serves 4		6 tbsp white wine	6 tbsp sour cream
		1 garlic clove, chopped	1 tbsp chopped fresh thyme
		1 tbsp chopped fresh thyme	
10–15 minutes + 3 hours to marinate		1 tbsp chopped fresh rosemary	GARNISH freshly grated Parmesan cheese
		4 skinless chicken breasts, cut into strips	sprigs of fresh rosemary
8–16 minutes		1 lb/450 g spaghetti	

To make the marinade, put all the ingredients into a large, shallow, glass dish and mix together well. Add the chicken and coat in the marinade. Cover with plastic wrap and refrigerate for 3 hours.

Bring a pan of lightly salted water to a boil and add the spaghetti. Cook over medium heat for about 10 minutes if using dried pasta, or 4 minutes if using fresh (check the instructions on the package), until tender but still firm to the bite. Meanwhile, lift the chicken out of the marinade, drain, and season. Discard the marinade. Heat the oil in a skillet, add the chicken, and cook over medium heat for 2–3 minutes on each side, or until cooked through.

In a bowl, mix the sour cream with the thyme. Drain the spaghetti and mix with half of the sour cream. Pile the spaghetti onto a large serving platter, then top with the chicken. Pour over the remaining sour cream, scatter over the Parmesan, garnish with rosemary sprigs, and serve.

lemon chicken with rice

		ingredients	
very easy		4 skinless chicken breasts, cut into bite-size chunks	2 garlic cloves, chopped
		salt and pepper	3 tbsp lemon oil
serves 4		4 tbsp butter	6 tbsp white wine
		1 garlic clove, chopped	1 tbsp chopped fresh cilantro
10–15 minutes + 3 hours to marinate		1 onion, thinly sliced	GARNISH
		juice and grated zest of 1 lemon	toasted slivered almonds
		½ cup chicken bouillon	fresh cilantro leaves
10 minutes		MARINADE	TO SERVE
		juice and grated zest of 1 lemon	freshly cooked rice
			selection of freshly cooked vegetables

To make the marinade, put all the ingredients into a large, shallow, glass dish and mix together well. Add the chicken and coat in the marinade. Cover with plastic wrap and refrigerate for 3 hours.

Lift out the chicken, drain well, and season. Discard the marinade. Heat the butter in a skillet, add the garlic and onion, and cook over low heat, stirring, for 2 minutes. Add the lemon juice and zest, bouillon, and chicken and bring to a boil. Lower the heat to medium and cook for 7–8 minutes, or until cooked through.

Arrange the cooked rice on a large serving platter. Remove the pan from the heat and place the chicken mixture over the rice. Scatter over the almonds and cilantro leaves. Serve with a selection of freshly cooked vegetables.

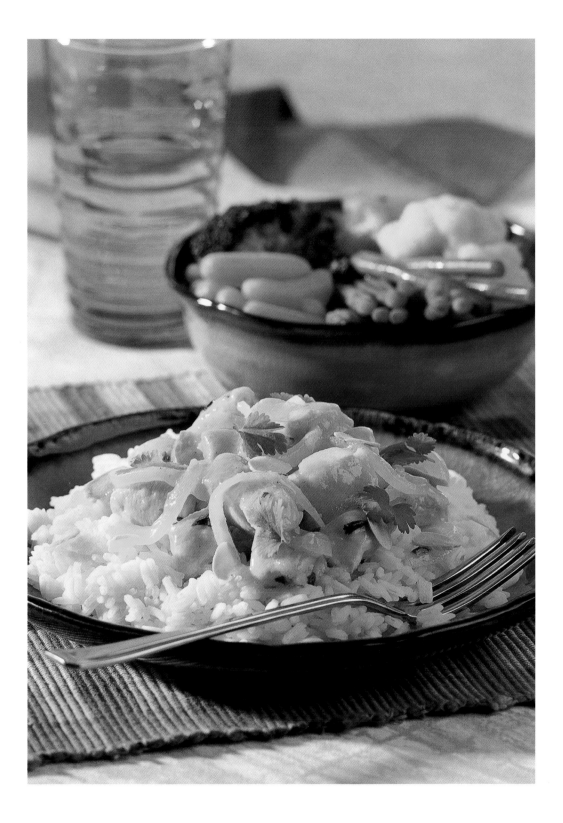

chicken in cranberry & red wine sauce

		ingredients	
easy		1¼ cups chicken bouillon 4 skinless, boneless chicken breasts 1 bay leaf salt and pepper	1 tbsp chopped fresh thyme salt and pepper
serves 4			CRANBERRY & RED WINE SAUCE 1¾ cups fresh cranberries
20 minutes		LEMON POTATOES 1 lb 5 oz/600 g small new potatoes, scrubbed 2 garlic cloves, chopped	½ cup superfine sugar 1¼ cups red wine
1 hour 25 minutes		3 tbsp olive oil juice of ½ lemon	sprigs of fresh thyme, to garnish

Preheat the oven to 400°F/200°C. Arrange the potatoes in a roasting pan. Put the garlic, oil, lemon juice, and chopped thyme into a bowl, season, and mix well. Pour the mixture over the potatoes and turn the potatoes until thoroughly coated. Roast in the preheated oven for 50 minutes, basting occasionally, until golden brown and tender.

Halfway through the cooking time, pour the bouillon into a pan and bring to a boil. Add the chicken and bay leaf, reduce the heat, and simmer for about 20 minutes, until cooked through. To make the sauce, put all the ingredients into a pan and bring to a boil. Reduce the heat and simmer, stirring occasionally, for 15 minutes, until thickened. Lift out the chicken and discard the bay leaf. Slice the chicken and arrange on 4 serving plates. Remove the potatoes from the oven and divide between the plates. Spoon over the sauce, garnish with thyme, and serve.

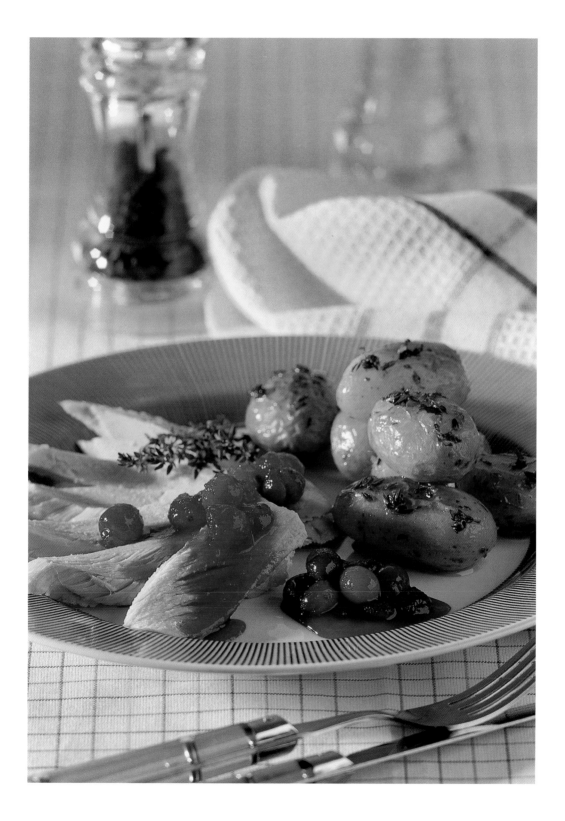

sweet & sour chicken

very easy	**ingredients**	
serves 4	4 skinless chicken breasts salt and pepper 1/2 cup all-purpose flour 2 tbsp olive oil 2 large garlic cloves, chopped 1 bay leaf 1 tbsp grated fresh gingerroot 1 tbsp chopped fresh lemongrass 4 tbsp sherry vinegar 5 tbsp rice wine or sherry 1 tbsp honey	1 tsp chili powder 1/2 cup orange juice 4 tbsp lime juice TO GARNISH toasted slivered almonds wedges of lime TO SERVE sautéed sliced potatoes carrots, cut into sticks and freshly cooked
15 minutes		
40–45 minutes		

Season the chicken breasts on both sides with salt and pepper, then roll them in the flour until coated. Heat the olive oil in a large skillet. Add the garlic and cook, stirring, over medium heat for 1 minute. Add the chicken, bay leaf, gingerroot, and lemongrass and cook for 2 minutes on each side.

Add the vinegar, rice wine, and honey, bring to a boil, then lower the heat and simmer, stirring occasionally, for 10 minutes. Add the chili powder, then stir in the orange juice and lime juice. Simmer for another 10 minutes. Using a perforated spoon, lift out the chicken and set aside. Strain and reserve the liquid and discard the bay leaf, then return the liquid to the pan with the chicken. Simmer for another 15–20 minutes.

Remove from the heat and transfer to individual serving plates. Garnish with toasted slivered almonds and lime wedges, and serve with sautéed sliced potatoes and freshly cooked carrots.

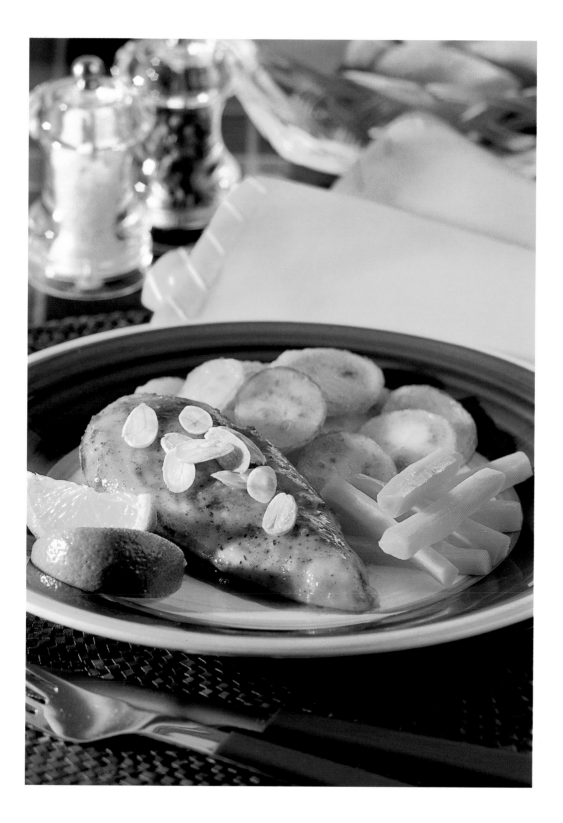

stuffed chicken breasts
with herbs

		ingredients	
easy		4 tbsp butter	salt and pepper
		1 onion, finely chopped	4 large, skinless chicken breasts
serves 4		4 strips smoked lean	
		bacon, chopped	TO GARNISH
		1 lb/450 g Swiss cheese, grated	toasted pine nuts
		1 egg, lightly beaten	sprigs of fresh basil
15 minutes		1 tbsp chopped fresh sage	
		2 tbsp chopped fresh basil	freshly cooked paglia e fieno, or other
			pasta ribbons, to serve
35 minutes			

Preheat the oven to 350°F/180°C. Melt half of the butter in a skillet over medium heat. Add the onion and cook, stirring, for 2 minutes. Add the bacon and cook for another 2 minutes. Remove from the heat and transfer to a large bowl. Add the cheese, egg, and herbs to the bowl. Season with salt and pepper and mix together well.

Halve each chicken breast and pound lightly to flatten each piece. Spoon some bacon mixture into the center of each piece, roll up, and secure with toothpicks. Transfer to a large roasting dish and dot with the remaining butter. Bake in the preheated oven for 30 minutes until golden.

Divide the freshly cooked pasta between 4 serving plates. Remove the chicken from the oven and place 2 chicken rolls on top of each bed of pasta. Garnish with toasted pine nuts and sprigs of fresh basil and serve.

entrées

Chicken is popular in cooking all over the world. This section presents a spectacular array of exciting and satisfying dishes from different countries, such as Italian Pesto Chicken, and Coq au Vin from France. There is also a Fiery Chicken Vindaloo, which takes its inspiration from India. And what could demonstrate chicken's marvelous versatility better than Mexican Chicken with Chile Chocolate Sauce? Mexican cooks have been pairing rich chocolate with hot chiles for centuries, and the flavor of chicken complements this combination perfectly.

roast chicken with hazelnut stuffing

		ingredients	
easy	3 tbsp butter, softened	1 tbsp olive oil	
	1 garlic clove, finely chopped	generous 1¾ cups sherry	
serves 4	3 tbsp finely chopped toasted hazelnuts	1 tsp ground cumin	
	1 tbsp grated lemon zest	1 heaping tsp cornstarch	
15 minutes + 10 minutes to rest	1 tbsp chopped fresh flatleaf parsley	TO GARNISH slices of lemon	
	salt and pepper	sprigs of fresh flatleaf parsley	
	1 medium oven-ready chicken, about 4 lb/1.8 kg	TO SERVE	
1 hour 45 minutes	1 lemon, cut into fourths	roast potatoes selection of freshly cooked vegetables	

Preheat the oven to 375°F/190°C. Mix 1 tablespoon of the butter with the garlic, hazelnuts, lemon zest, and parsley. Season well. Loosen the chicken skin from the breast without breaking it. Push the butter mixture evenly between the skin and breast meat. Put the lemon wedges inside the body cavity.

Pour the olive oil into a roasting pan. Put the chicken in it. Pour over the sherry, season, rub the skin with cumin, and dot with the remaining butter. Roast for 1 hour 40 minutes, basting occasionally, until cooked through. Check it is cooked by inserting a knife into the thick part of a thigh—the juices should run clear. Lift out onto a serving plate to rest for 10 minutes. Mix the cornstarch with 2 tablespoons of water, then stir into the juices in the pan. Transfer to the stove. Stir over low heat until thickened. Add more water if necessary. Garnish the chicken with lemon slices and parsley. Serve with potatoes, vegetables, and the cooking sauce.

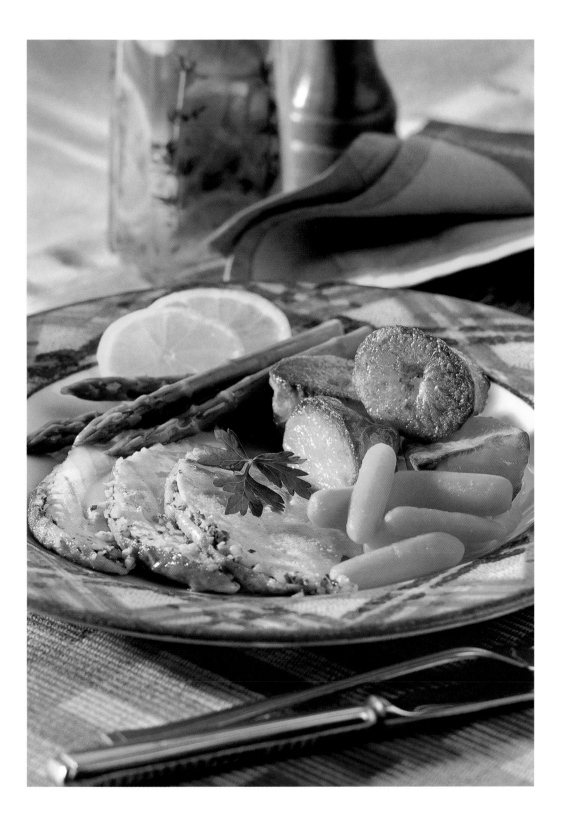

honey-glazed chicken

easy	
serves 4	
15 minutes + 10 minutes to rest	
1 hour 45 minutes	

ingredients

3 tbsp clear honey

$\frac{1}{2}$ tsp salt

1 tsp powdered mustard

1 tbsp light soy sauce

1 tbsp olive oil

1 medium oven-ready chicken, about 4 lb/1.8 kg

1 orange, cut into fourths

$\frac{2}{3}$ cup chicken bouillon

1 tsp cornstarch

$\frac{2}{3}$ cup red wine

$\frac{2}{3}$ cup light cream

seedless red grapes, cut in half, to garnish

freshly cooked white rice and wild rice, to serve

Preheat the oven to 375°F/190°C. Put the honey, salt, mustard, and soy sauce into a bowl and mix well. Pour the olive oil into a roasting pan and place the chicken in it. Put the orange wedges inside the body cavity. Pour over the bouillon, then spread over the honey mixture. Roast for 1 hour 40 minutes, basting occasionally, until golden and cooked through. To check it is cooked, insert a knife into a thickest part of the thigh—the juices should run clear. Lift out the chicken and let rest for 10 minutes.

Mix the cornstarch with 1–2 tablespoons of water, then stir into the juices in the roasting pan. Transfer to the stove and stir over low heat for 1 minute, then pour in the wine. Bring to a boil, lower the heat, and cook, stirring, for 1 minute. Remove from the heat and stir in the cream. Arrange the cooked mixed rice on a serving platter, then place the chicken on it. Garnish with grapes and serve with the red wine sauce.

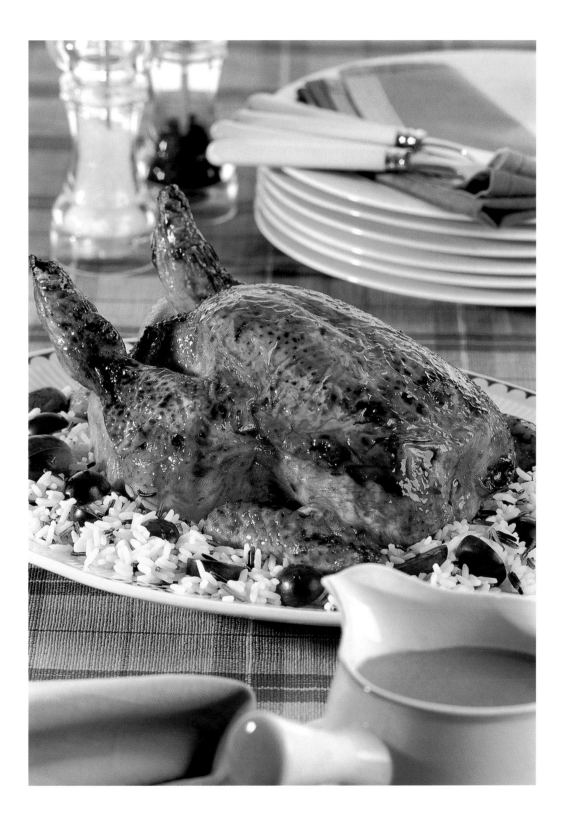

herb chicken with
white wine & vegetables

easy	
serves 4	
15 minutes + 10 minutes to rest	
1 hour 45 minutes	

ingredients

2 garlic cloves, finely chopped
1 tbsp chopped fresh
    flatleaf parsley
1 tbsp chopped fresh thyme
salt and pepper
1 medium oven-ready chicken,
    about 1.8 kg/4 lb
2 shallots, cut in half
1 lemon, cut into fourths

1 bay leaf
1 tbsp olive oil
$1\frac{1}{4}$ cups white wine
1 tbsp cornstarch

sprigs of fresh thyme, to garnish

TO SERVE
roast potatoes
selection of freshly cooked vegetables
gravy

Preheat the oven to 375°F/190°C. Put the garlic, parsley, and thyme into a bowl and mix well. Season well. Loosen the chicken skin from the breast without breaking it. Push the mixture evenly between the skin and breast meat. Put the shallots, lemon wedges, and bay leaf inside the body cavity.

Pour the oil into a roasting pan and place the chicken in it. Pour over half of the wine. Roast for 1 hour 40 minutes, basting occasionally, until golden and cooked through. Check it is cooked by inserting a knife into the thickest part of a thigh—the juices should run clear. Lift out the chicken and let rest for 10 minutes.

Mix the cornstarch with 1–2 tablespoons of water, then stir into the juices in the pan. Transfer to the stove and stir over low heat for 1 minute. Stir in the remaining wine. Bring to a boil, lower the heat, and cook, stirring, for 1 minute. Cut the chicken into slices, garnish with thyme, and serve with roast potatoes, vegetables, and gravy.

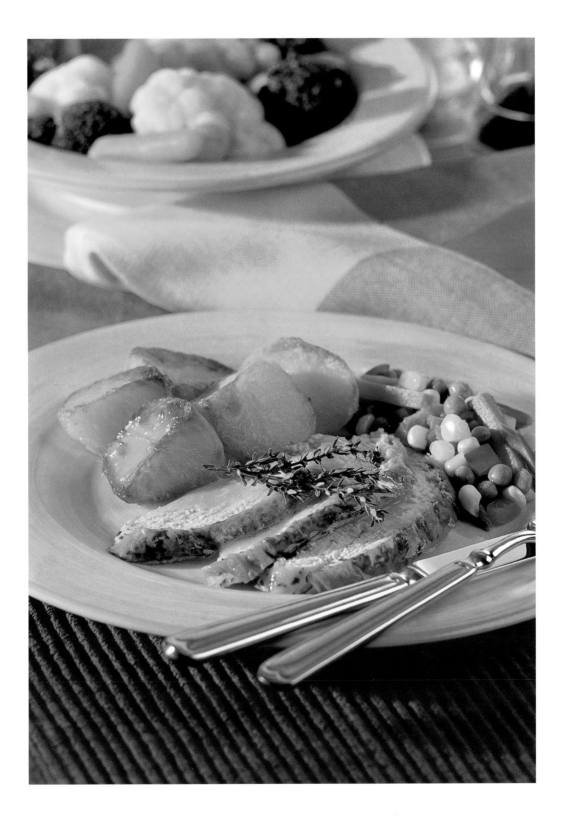

italian pesto chicken

		ingredients	
very easy		**PESTO** 1 oz/25 g fresh basil, thick 　stems removed generous 1¼ cups pine nuts 3 garlic cloves, coarsely chopped scant ½ cup extra-virgin olive oil ¾ cup freshly grated Parmesan cheese salt and pepper	2¾ oz/75 g sun-dried tomatoes in olive 　oil, drained and chopped 2 tbsp extra-virgin olive oil ½ cup white wine 7 oz/200 g canned chopped tomatoes
serves 4			**GARNISH** black olives, pitted and halved sprigs of fresh basil
15–20 minutes		4 skinless chicken breasts 8 slices prosciutto	freshly cooked linguine, to serve
30 minutes			

Preheat the oven to 350°F/180°C. To make the pesto, put all the ingredients into a food processor and season with salt and pepper. Blend for a few seconds until smooth.

Halve each chicken breast and pound lightly to flatten each piece. Spread on one side only with pesto, then top with the prosciutto. Add a tablespoon of sun-dried tomatoes to each one, then roll them up and secure with toothpicks.

Pour the olive oil into a large roasting pan. Arrange the chicken in the pan, then pour over the wine. Add the chopped tomatoes and bake in the preheated oven for 30 minutes.

Stir any remaining pesto into the cooked pasta and arrange on 4 serving plates. Remove the chicken from the oven, discard the toothpicks and slice in half, widthwise. Divide between the plates. Pour over some of the cooking sauce, garnish with black olives and sprigs of basil, and serve.

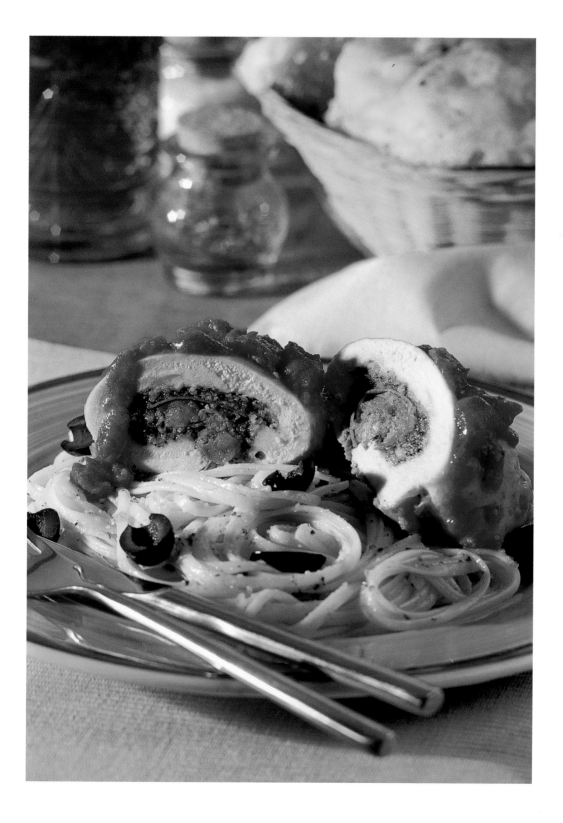

fiery chicken vindaloo

		ingredients	
	very easy	1 tsp ground cumin	4 skinless chicken breasts, cut into bite-size chunks
	serves 4	1 tsp ground cinnamon 2 tsp mustard powder 1½ tsp ground coriander 1 tsp cayenne pepper	2 small red chiles, seeded and chopped 1 lb/450 g potatoes, peeled and chopped 1 lb 12 oz/800 g canned chopped tomatoes
	15 minutes	5 tbsp red wine vinegar 1 tsp brown sugar ⅔ cup vegetable oil 8 garlic cloves, crushed	1 tbsp tomato paste a few drops of red food coloring salt and pepper
	1 hour 10 minutes	3 red onions, sliced	freshly boiled rice, to serve

Put the cumin, cinnamon, mustard, ground coriander, and cayenne pepper into a bowl. Add the vinegar and sugar and mix well.

Heat the oil in a large skillet. Add the garlic and onions and cook, stirring, over medium heat for 5 minutes. Add the chicken and cook for another 3 minutes, then add the chiles, potatoes, chopped tomatoes and tomato paste, and a few drops of red food coloring. Stir in the spice mixture, season generously with salt and pepper, and bring to a boil. Lower the heat, cover the pan, and simmer, stirring occasionally, for 1 hour.

Arrange the cooked rice on a large serving platter. Remove the pan from the heat, spoon the chicken mixture over the rice, and serve.

mexican chicken with chile chocolate sauce

		ingredients
very easy	2 tbsp chili oil 1 garlic clove, chopped 4 skinless chicken breasts 1 onion, chopped 1 red bell pepper, skinned, seeded, and chopped 1 large tomato, skinned, seeded, and chopped 1 small red chile, seeded and chopped 1 tbsp unsweetened cocoa generous 2 cups chicken bouillon	generous $\frac{1}{3}$ cup raisins scant $\frac{1}{2}$ cup pine nuts 1 tsp ground allspice 1 tsp brown sugar $1\frac{3}{4}$ oz/50 g semisweet chocolate, broken into small pieces scant $\frac{1}{2}$ cup red wine juice of $\frac{1}{2}$ orange freshly cooked rice or potatoes, to serve

- very easy
- serves 4
- 15–20 minutes
- 1 hour

Heat the oil in a flameproof casserole. Add the garlic and cook, stirring, over medium heat for 3 minutes. Add the chicken and cook for 3 minutes, then turn over and cook on the other side for another 2 minutes. Lift out the chicken, cut into bite-size chunks, and set aside.

Preheat the oven to 350°F/180°C. Add the onion, red bell pepper, tomato, chile, and unsweetened cocoa to the pan. Cook, stirring, for 5 minutes. Then add the bouillon, raisins, pine nuts, allspice, and sugar and cook for 2 minutes. Return the chicken to the casserole. Add the chocolate and stir until melted, then stir in the red wine and orange juice. Bring to a boil then remove from the heat.

Transfer to the preheated oven and bake for about 40 minutes or until cooked through. Remove from the oven and serve with freshly cooked rice or potatoes.

sweet chicken pie

		ingredients	
	easy	**PIE DOUGH**	3 tbsp brandy
		2½ cups all-purpose flour, plus extra	1 tbsp raisins
		for dusting	1¾ oz/50 g hazelnuts, toasted
	serves 4	pinch of salt	and ground
		¾ cup butter, chopped, plus extra	½ cup grated colby cheese
	20 minutes	for greasing	1 tsp ground allspice
	+ 1 hour	about 6 tbsp cold water	salt and pepper
	to chill		
		1 cup chicken bouillon	TO SERVE
	1¼ hours	1 lb 9 oz/700 g boneless chicken,	freshly cooked potatoes
		cut into bite-size chunks	selection of freshly cooked vegetables
		1 egg, lightly beaten	seedless white grapes, halved, optional

To make the dough, mix the flour and salt in a bowl. Rub in the butter to form fine crumbs. Gradually mix in enough cold water to make a pliable dough. Knead lightly. Wrap in plastic wrap and chill in the refrigerator for 1 hour. Meanwhile, pour the bouillon into a pan and bring to a boil. Lower the heat, add the chicken, and cook for 30 minutes. Remove from the heat, cool for 25 minutes, then transfer to a bowl. Stir in the remaining ingredients. Season.

Preheat the oven to 375°F/190°C. Grease a 9-inch/23-cm pie pan with butter. Remove the dough from the refrigerator. On a floured counter, shape half into a ball, roll out to a thickness of ¼ inch/ 5 mm, and use it to line the pan. Spoon in the chicken filling, then roll out the remaining dough. Moisten the pie rim with water, cover the pie with the remaining dough, and trim the edges. Cut 2 slits in the top and add dough leaf shapes made from trimmings. Brush with the egg. Bake for 45 minutes. Serve with potatoes, vegetables, and grapes if using.

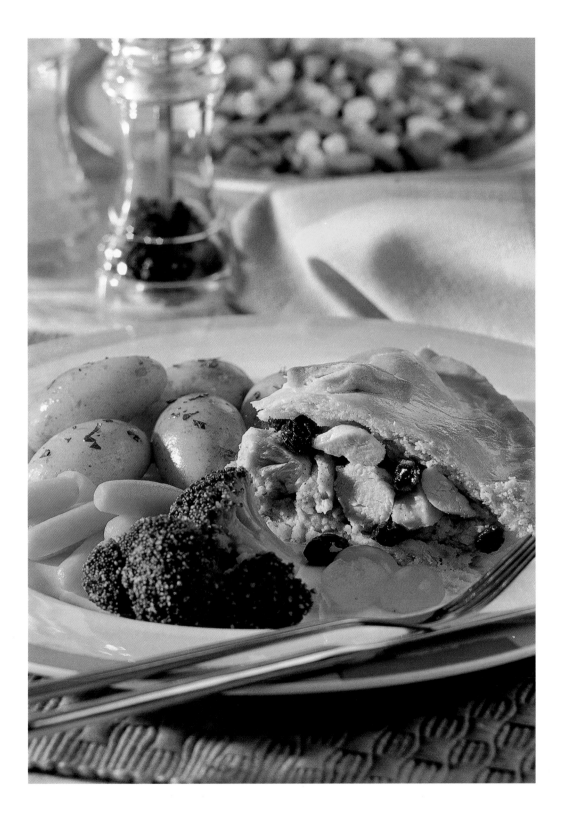

coq au vin

		ingredients	
very easy			
serves 4	2 tbsp butter	1 bouquet garni	
	8 baby onions	1 tbsp chopped fresh tarragon	
	4½ oz/125 g lean bacon,	salt and pepper	
	coarsely chopped	2 tsp cornstarch	
15 minutes	4 fresh chicken joints		
	1 garlic clove, finely chopped	sprigs of fresh flatleaf parsley,	
	12 white mushrooms	to garnish	
	1¼ cups red wine		
1 hour 10 minutes		sautéed sliced potatoes, to serve	

Melt half of the butter in a large skillet over medium heat. Add the onions and bacon and cook, stirring, for 3 minutes. Lift out the bacon and onions and set aside. Melt the remaining butter in the pan and add the chicken. Cook for 3 minutes, then turn over and cook on the other side for 2 minutes. Drain off any excess chicken fat. Return the bacon and onions to the pan, then add the garlic, mushrooms, red wine, and herbs. Season with salt and pepper. Cook for about 1 hour, or until cooked through. Remove from the heat, lift out the chicken, onions, bacon, and mushrooms, transfer them to a serving platter, and keep warm. Discard the bouquet garni.

Mix the cornstarch with 1–2 tablespoons of water, then stir it into the juices in the pan. Bring to a boil, lower the heat, and cook, stirring, for 1 minute. Pour the sauce over the chicken, garnish with sprigs of parsley, and serve with sautéed sliced potatoes.

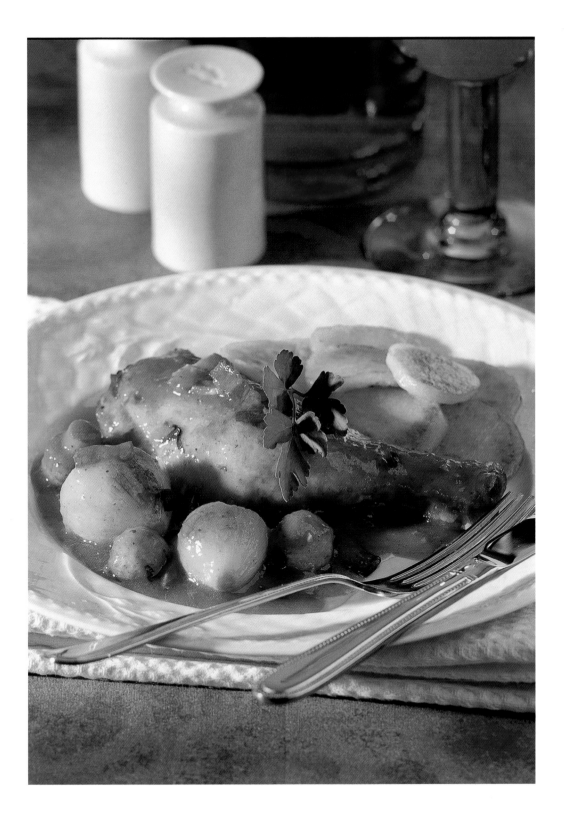

chicken & barley stew

		ingredients	
	very easy	2 tbsp vegetable oil	1 tbsp tomato paste
		8 small, skinless chicken thighs	1 bay leaf
	serves 4	generous 2 cups chicken bouillon	1 zucchini, trimmed and sliced
		scant $\frac{1}{2}$ cup pearl barley, rinsed	2 tbsp chopped fresh parsley
		and drained	2 tbsp all-purpose flour
		7 oz/200 g small new potatoes,	salt and pepper
	15 minutes	scrubbed and cut in half, lengthwise	
		2 large carrots, peeled and sliced	sprigs of fresh flatleaf parsley,
		1 leek, trimmed and sliced	to garnish
	1 hour	2 shallots, sliced	fresh crusty bread, to serve

Heat the oil in a large pot over medium heat. Add the chicken and cook for 3 minutes, then turn over and cook on the other side for another 2 minutes. Add the bouillon, barley, potatoes, carrots, leek, shallots, tomato paste, and the bay leaf. Bring to a boil, lower the heat, and simmer for 30 minutes. Add the zucchini and parsley, cover the pan, and cook for another 20 minutes, or until the chicken is cooked through. Remove the bay leaf and discard.

In a separate bowl, mix the flour with 4 tablespoons of water and stir into a smooth paste. Add it to the stew and cook, stirring, over low heat for another 5 minutes. Remove from the heat, ladle into individual serving bowls, and garnish with sprigs of fresh parsley. Serve with fresh crusty bread.

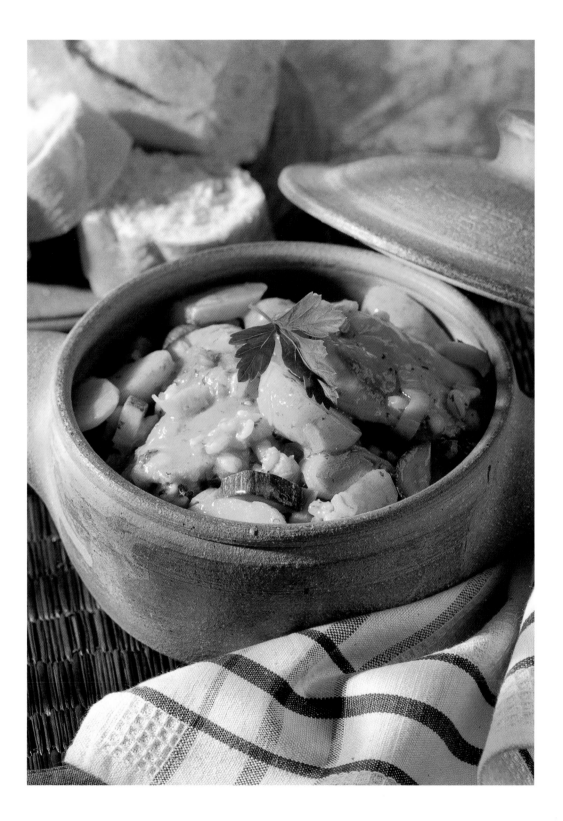

chicken & vegetable bake

		ingredients	
very easy		FILLING	TOPPING
		1¼ cups chicken bouillon	2 lb/900 g potatoes, peeled, cooked,
		1 lb/450 g boneless chicken, chopped	and mashed
serves 4		3½ oz/100 g white mushrooms	1 onion, grated
		1 tbsp butter, for greasing	1 cup grated colby cheese
		1 tbsp cornstarch	
		⅔ cup milk	sprigs of fresh rosemary, to garnish
15 minutes		7 oz/200 g carrots, peeled, blanched,	
		and chopped	selection of freshly cooked vegetables,
		1 tbsp chopped fresh rosemary	to serve
1 hour		salt and pepper	

To make the filling, pour the bouillon into a large pan and bring to a boil. Add the chicken and mushrooms, lower the heat, cover the pan, and simmer for 25–30 minutes. Grease a 2-pint/1.2-litre ovenproof pie pan with butter. Remove the pan from the heat. Lift out the chicken and mushrooms and place in the prepared pie pan. Reserve the bouillon.

Preheat the oven to 400°F/200°C. In a bowl, mix the cornstarch with enough of the milk to make a smooth paste, then stir in the remaining milk. Stir into the bouillon. Pour the mixture into the pie pan, add the carrots and rosemary, and season well. To make the topping, put the mashed potatoes into a bowl. Add the grated onion and half of the cheese, and mix well. Spoon the mixture over the chicken filling, level the surface, then scatter over the remaining cheese. Bake for 30 minutes until golden. Remove from the oven, garnish with rosemary, and serve with vegetables.

chicken risotto

		ingredients	
easy		4 tbsp butter	5 cups hot chicken bouillon
		1 onion, chopped	2¾ oz/75 g crimini mushrooms, sliced
serves 4		4½ oz/125 g skinless chicken breasts, chopped	1¾ oz/50 g cashews, broken in half
		12 oz/350 g risotto rice	TO GARNISH
10–15 minutes		1 tsp turmeric	shavings of fresh Parmesan cheese
		salt and pepper	fresh basil leaves
		1¼ cups white wine	fresh arugula, to serve
45–50 minutes			

Melt the butter in a large pan over medium heat. Add the onion and cook, stirring, for 1 minute. Add the chicken and cook, stirring, for another 5 minutes.

Add the rice and cook, stirring, for 15 minutes. Then add the turmeric, season with salt and pepper, and mix well. Gradually stir in the wine, then stir in the hot bouillon, a ladleful at a time, waiting for each ladleful to be absorbed before stirring in the next. Simmer for 20 minutes, stirring from time to time, until the rice is tender and nearly all of the liquid has been absorbed. If necessary, add a little more bouillon to prevent the risotto from drying out. Stir in the mushrooms and cashews, and cook for another 3 minutes.

Arrange the arugula on 4 individual serving plates. Remove the risotto from the heat and spoon it over the arugula. Scatter over the Parmesan shavings and basil leaves and serve at once.

entertaining

The versatility of chicken makes it the ideal
food for entertaining, and this section
presents a delicious range of recipes for
barbecues, buffets, and dinner parties. Your
guests will find the Barbecued Tandoori
Chicken irresistible, while the Chicken
Pinwheels with Blue Cheese & Herbs will
invite many admiring comments. Children
will love the Crispy Chicken Burgers, and
the elegant Poached Chicken with Brandy
& Cream will linger in the memory long
after your guests have eaten it.

grilled tandoori chicken

		ingredients	
	very easy	**MARINADE**	**SKEWERS**
		scant 2 cups plain yogurt	6 skinless chicken breasts
		4 tbsp lime juice	1 red bell pepper, seeded
	serves 4	2 garlic cloves, crushed	1 green bell pepper, seeded
		1 tsp salt	16 baby onions
	15 minutes + 2 hours to marinate	pinch of saffron threads	
		1 tsp ground coriander	**TO GARNISH**
		1 tsp ground cumin	lime wedges
		1 tsp ground ginger	fresh cilantro leaves
	15–20 minutes	½ tsp chili powder	
		pepper	freshly steamed or boiled rice, to serve

To make the marinade, put the yogurt, lime juice, garlic, salt, and
spices into a large, shallow, nonmetallic (glass or ceramic) bowl,
which will not react with acid. Season with plenty of pepper and
mix together well.

Cut the chicken and bell peppers into bite-size pieces and thread
onto 8 skewers, alternating with the onions. When the skewers are
full (leave a small space at either end), put them in the bowl and
turn in the marinade until they are coated. Cover with plastic wrap
and place in the refrigerator to marinate for at least 2 hours.

Lift the skewers out of the marinade. Grill over hot coals or cook
under a hot broiler for 15–20 minutes, or until cooked right
through, turning them frequently and basting with the remaining
marinade. Remove from the heat, arrange on a bed of freshly
cooked rice, garnish with fresh cilantro leaves, and serve.

chicken pitas

		ingredients	
very easy		4 tbsp lemon juice	7 oz/200 g kalamata olives, pitted
		2 garlic cloves, crushed	and cut in half
serves 4		1 tsp dried oregano	
		1 tbsp honey	DRESSING
		1 small red chile, seeded and	1 tbsp lemon juice
15–20 minutes + 2 hours to marinate		finely chopped	15 tbsp extra-virgin olive oil
		salt and pepper	2 tbsp white wine vinegar
		6 skinless chicken breasts, cut into	½ tsp sugar
		bite-size pieces	2 tbsp chopped fresh cilantro
15–20 minutes		4 tomatoes, sliced	fresh cilantro leaves, to garnish
		1 red onion, sliced	8 small pitas, warmed, to serve

Put the lemon juice, garlic, oregano, honey, and chile into a large, shallow, nonmetallic (glass or ceramic) bowl, which will not react with acid. Season with plenty of salt and pepper and mix well. Add the chicken pieces to the bowl and turn them in the marinade until they are coated. Cover with plastic wrap and place in the refrigerator to marinate for at least 2 hours.

Lift the chicken breasts out of the marinade. Grill over hot coals or cook under a hot broiler for 15–20 minutes, or until cooked right through, turning them frequently and basting with the remaining marinade. While they are cooking, make the dressing. Put all the ingredients into a screw-top jar and shake well, or put them into a bowl and mix together. Put the tomatoes, onion, and olives into a separate bowl and drizzle over the dressing. Divide the salad between 8 split pitas and add the cooked chicken. Garnish with cilantro leaves and serve.

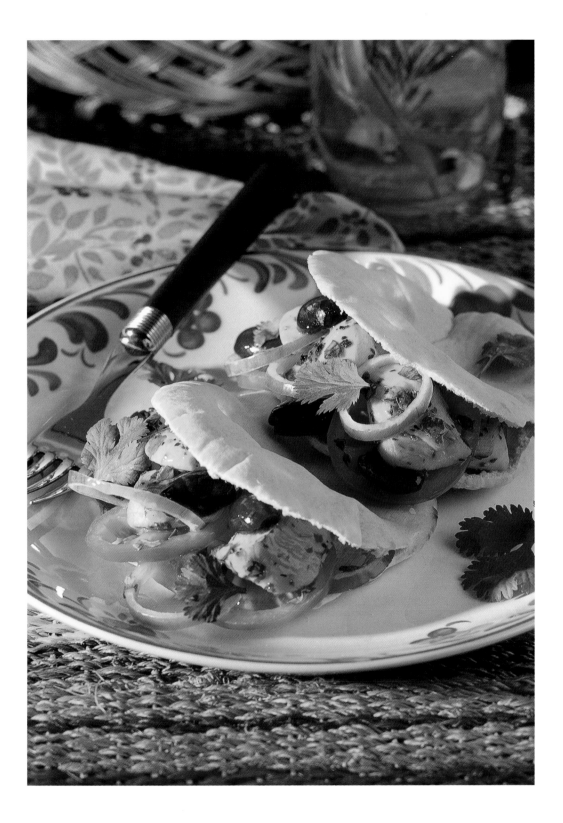

chicken & mushroom kabobs

very easy	
serves 4	
15 minutes + 2 hours to marinate	
15–20 minutes	

ingredients

MARINADE
½ cup extra-virgin olive oil
2 garlic cloves, crushed
1 tbsp dried basil
1 tbsp dried thyme
salt and pepper

6 skinless chicken breasts, cut into
    bite-size pieces
16 white mushrooms

8 baby onions
8 cherry tomatoes

sprigs of fresh rosemary, to garnish

TO SERVE
fresh salad greens
chopped cucumber
long sprigs of fresh rosemary to use as
    skewers, optional

To make the marinade, put the oil, garlic, basil, and thyme into a large, shallow bowl. Season with salt and pepper and mix well.

Thread the chicken pieces onto 8 skewers (or rosemary skewers, if using), alternating them with the mushrooms, onions, and cherry tomatoes. When the skewers are full (leave a small space at either end), put them into the bowl, and turn them in the marinade until they are well coated. Cover with plastic wrap and place in the refrigerator to marinate for at least 2 hours.

Lift the skewers out of the marinade. Grill over hot coals or cook under a hot broiler for 15–20 minutes, or until cooked right through, turning them frequently and basting with the remaining marinade. Remove from the heat, arrange the skewers on a bed of fresh salad greens and chopped cucumber, garnish with sprigs of fresh rosemary, and serve.

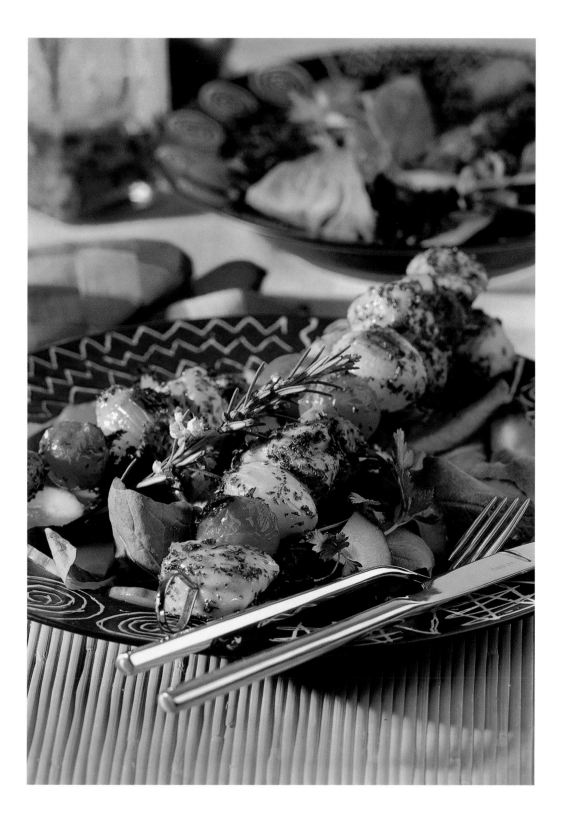

sweet & sour chicken drumsticks

		ingredients	
very easy		MARINADE	8 chicken drumsticks
		4 tbsp sherry vinegar	
serves 4		2 tbsp light soy sauce	4 long, red chiles, made into flowers
		3 garlic cloves, crushed	(see below), to garnish
		2 tbsp honey	
15 minutes		2 tbsp tomato paste	arugula leaves, to serve
+ 2 hours		1 tsp paprika	
to marinate		salt and pepper	
15–20 minutes			

To make the marinade, put the vinegar, soy sauce, garlic, honey, tomato paste, and paprika into a large, shallow, nonmetallic (glass or ceramic) bowl, which will not react with acid. Season with salt and pepper and mix well. Add the chicken drumsticks to the bowl and turn in the marinade until well coated. Cover with plastic wrap and place in the refrigerator to marinate for at least 2 hours. Meanwhile, make the chile flowers. Using a sharp knife, make 6 slits about ½ inch/1 cm in length from the stem end to the tip of each chile. Put them in a bowl of iced water and soak for at least 30 minutes until they have expanded into flower shapes.

Lift the drumsticks out of the marinade. Grill over hot coals or cook under a hot broiler for 15–20 minutes, or until cooked through, turning them frequently and basting with the remaining marinade. Arrange the arugula on a large serving platter and pile the cooked drumsticks on top. Garnish with the chile flowers and serve.

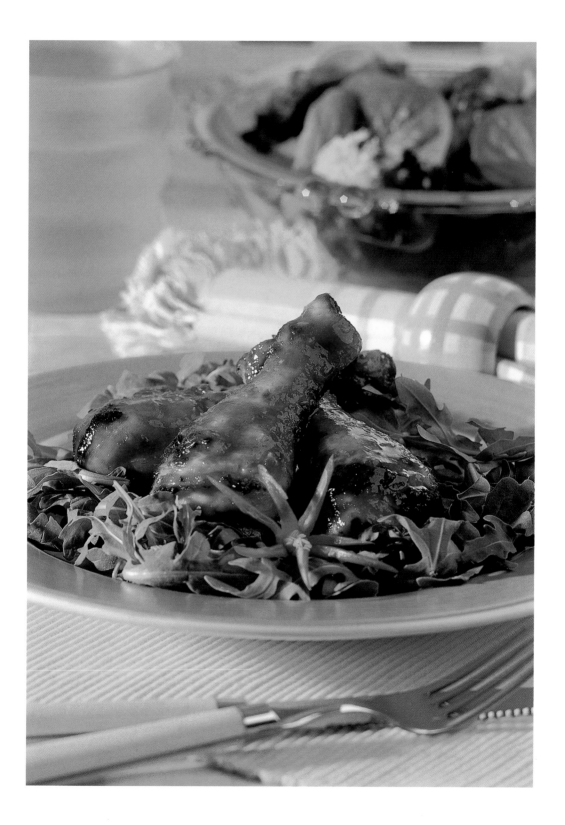

honey-glazed chicken skewers

		ingredients	
very easy		6 skinless chicken breasts, cut into bite-size pieces	HONEY GLAZE
		16 white mushrooms	2 tbsp white wine vinegar
serves 4		3 red onions, cut into bite-size pieces	¾ cup honey
		2 red bell peppers, seeded and cut into bite-size pieces	1 tbsp prepared mustard
15 minutes		2 zucchini, trimmed and cut into bite-size pieces	1 tbsp soy sauce
			2 tbsp cornstarch
20–25 minutes			fresh flatleaf parsley, to garnish
			mixture of freshly cooked white rice and wild rice, to serve

Thread the chicken pieces onto 8 skewers, alternating with the mushrooms, onions, red bell peppers, and zucchini (leave a small space at either end).

To make the honey glaze, put the vinegar, honey, mustard, and soy sauce into a small pan and bring to a boil. Meanwhile, in a bowl, mix the cornstarch with enough water to make a smooth paste. When the honey mixture has reached boiling point, lower the heat, stir in the cornstarch mixture, and simmer gently for 1 minute. Remove from the heat.

Brush the honey glaze over the chicken skewers until they are well coated. Grill over hot coals or cook under a hot broiler for 15–20 minutes, or until cooked right through, turning them frequently and basting with the remaining honey glaze. Remove from the heat, arrange on a bed of freshly cooked white rice and wild rice, garnish with fresh parsley, and serve.

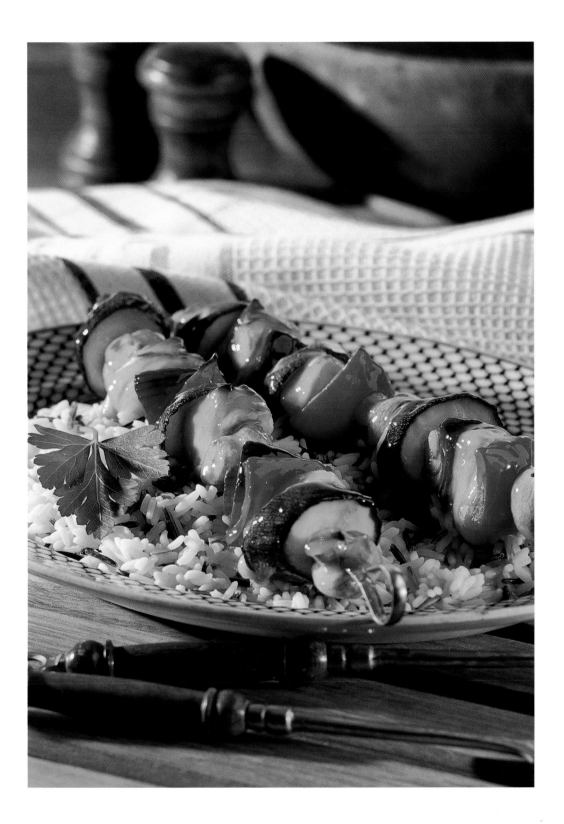

mexican citrus chicken

		ingredients	
very easy	MARINADE	1 tbsp red wine vinegar
	1 small red chile, seeded	1 garlic clove, crushed
serves 4	4 tbsp lime juice	6 tomatoes, coarsely chopped
	1 tbsp orange juice	3 scallions, trimmed and sliced
	4 tbsp extra-virgin olive oil	2 tbsp chopped fresh flatleaf parsley
20 minutes + 2 hours to marinate	1 tbsp tequila	sprigs of fresh mint, to garnish
	4 skinless chicken breasts	8 small flour tortillas, warmed, to serve
15–20 minutes	CITRUS SALSA	
	2 tbsp lime juice	
	2 tbsp orange juice	

To make the marinade, finely chop the chile and put in a large, shallow, nonmetallic (glass or ceramic) bowl with the citrus juices, olive oil, and tequila. Mix well. Halve each chicken breast and pound lightly to tenderize each piece. Add them to the bowl and turn in the marinade until coated. Cover with plastic wrap and place in the refrigerator to marinate for at least 2 hours.

About 30 minutes before the end of the marinating time, make the salsa. Put the lime juice, orange juice, vinegar, and garlic into a large bowl and mix together. Add the tomatoes, scallions, and chopped parsley and toss together until coated. Cover with plastic wrap and let stand for 30 minutes.

Lift the chicken out of the marinade. Grill over hot coals or cook under a hot broiler for 15–20 minutes, or until cooked through, turning frequently and basting with marinade. Divide the chicken and salsa between 8 tortillas, garnish with mint, and serve.

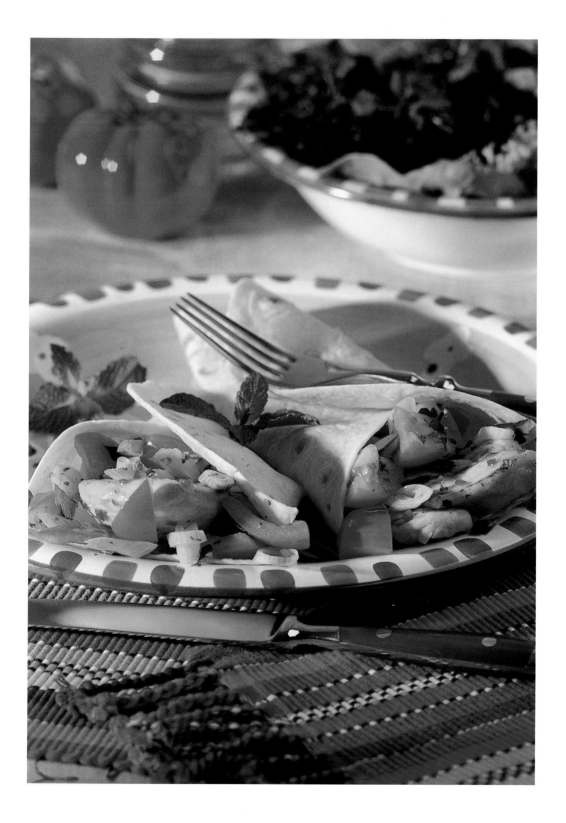

crispy chicken burgers

	ingredients	
easy	4½ cups fresh white or whole-wheat bread crumbs	1 tbsp chopped fresh thyme
		1 tbsp chopped fresh parsley
serves 4	8 oz/225 g cooked chicken meat, chopped	salt and pepper
	2 eggs	fresh salad greens, to garnish
15–20 minutes + 30 minutes to chill	1 onion, coarsely chopped	TO SERVE
	1 small red chile, seeded and chopped	hamburger buns
	1 large garlic clove, chopped	freshly sliced onion rings and
8–10 minutes	1 tbsp grated lemon zest	tomatoes, cooked or raw

Put 3 cups of the bread crumbs into a food processor with the chicken. Add one of the eggs, then all of the onion, chile, garlic, lemon zest, thyme, and parsley. Season well with salt and pepper, then blend until smooth. Transfer to a bowl, cover with plastic wrap, and refrigerate for 30 minutes.

Remove from the refrigerator and, using your hands, shape the mixture into burgers. Beat the remaining egg, then dip the burgers into the egg and coat with the remaining bread crumbs. Grill over hot coals or cook under a hot broiler for 4–5 minutes on each side, or until cooked right through.

Remove from the heat. Serve with hamburger buns and onion rings and tomatoes, garnished with fresh salad greens.

chicken pinwheels
with blue cheese & herbs

		ingredients	

	easy	2 tbsp pine nuts, lightly toasted
		2 tbsp chopped fresh parsley
		2 tbsp chopped fresh thyme
		1 garlic clove, chopped
		1 tbsp grated lemon zest
		salt and pepper
		4 large, skinless chicken breasts
		9 oz/250 g blue cheese, such as
		    Stilton, crumbled
			GARNISH
			twists of lemon
			sprigs of fresh thyme
			
			fresh green and red lettuce leaves,
			    to serve

	serves 4		
	15–20 minutes		
	10–12 minutes		

Put the pine nuts into a food processor with the parsley, thyme, garlic, and lemon zest. Season with salt and pepper.

Pound the chicken breasts lightly to flatten them. Spread them on one side with the pine nut mixture, then top with the cheese. Roll them up from one short end to the other, so that the filling is enclosed. Wrap the rolls individually in aluminum foil, and seal well. Transfer into a steamer, or a metal colander placed over a pan of boiling water, cover tightly, and steam for 10–12 minutes, or until cooked through.

Arrange the lettuce leaves on a large serving platter. Remove the chicken from the heat, discard the foil, and cut the chicken rolls into slices. Arrange the slices over the lettuce leaves, garnish with twists of lemon and sprigs of thyme, and serve.

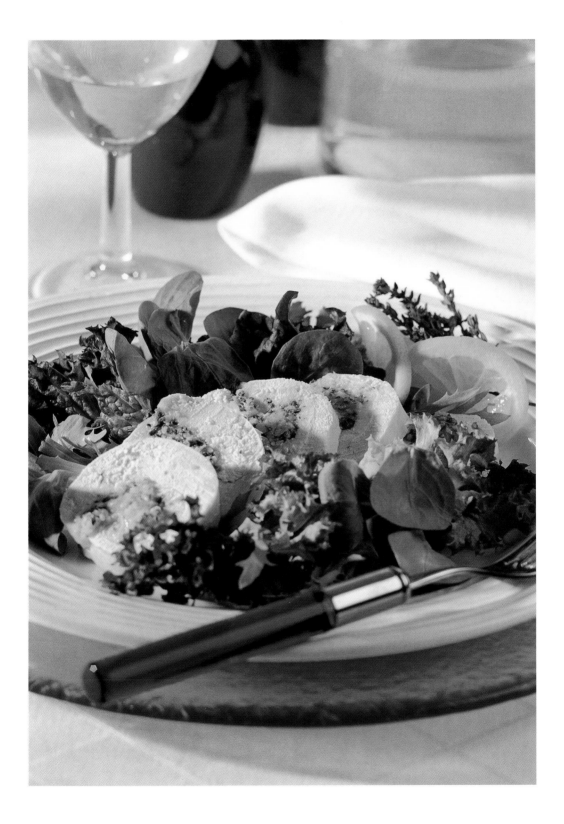

poached chicken
with brandy & cream

		ingredients	
very easy		1 tbsp butter	3 tbsp brandy
		1 garlic clove, chopped	salt and pepper
serves 4		2 onions, chopped	$2/3$ cup light cream
		scant 2 cups chicken bouillon	
		1 tbsp chopped fresh tarragon	GARNISH
		4 large, skinless chicken breasts	sprigs of fresh, flatleaf parsley
15 minutes		1 large tsp cornstarch	seedless white grapes, cut in half
		2 tbsp water	
			freshly cooked tagliatelle, to serve
17–20 minutes			

Melt the butter in a large pan over low heat. Add the garlic and onion and cook, stirring, for 3 minutes. Add the bouillon and half of the tarragon and bring to a boil. Lower the heat, add the chicken breasts, and cook for 10–12 minutes, or until cooked through.

Lift out the chicken, cut into slices, and keep warm. Strain the chicken bouillon and reserve. Discard the solids. In a separate large, heatproof bowl, mix the cornstarch with 2 tablespoons of water, then gradually stir in the bouillon. Return to the pan and cook gently for 1 minute, then pour in the brandy. Season with salt and pepper and the remaining tarragon. Bring to a boil, lower the heat, and cook, stirring, for 1 minute. Remove from the heat and stir in the cream.

Arrange the cooked pasta on a large serving platter. Arrange the chicken slices over the top and pour over the brandy sauce. Garnish with sprigs of parsley and white grapes and serve.

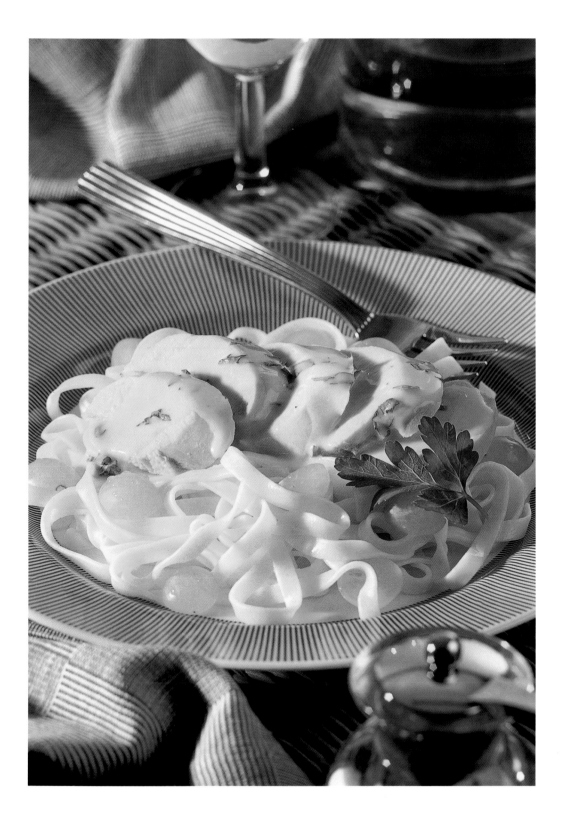

index